It's Godly To Be Rich

IT'S GODLY TO
BE RICH

Lionel M. Blair, Sr.

Contents

Acknowledgements

I would like to thank the greatest friend of all, my Lord and Savior Jesus Christ. Lord, without you I am nothing. I will always love and honor you above all. You amaze me every day! Thank you for reconciling me to the Father.

Also, I want to thank my wife, the lovely Jasmine Blair. Thank you for staying by my side. Your unconditional love means the world to me. I'm so grateful to God for you. Our love grows each year. I'm grateful to God for allowing me to share this journey called life with you. You make this journey fun.

Last, I want to thank all of my spiritual sons and daughters of IKAM. We could not do what we do without you all. Apostle Jasmine and I love you all so dearly. I thank you for the love and the bond we share. I absolutely love our growing family!

Special thanks to Apostle Ron Phillips, pastor emeritus of Abba's House in Chattanooga, Tennessee for forwarding this book. You have been an excellent father and mentor to Jasmine and I. We will love and cherish you forever.

Forward

Apostle Lionel Blair's powerful new book will bless many and disturb some! The powerful title," It's Godly to be Rich " will be a strong challenge to much erroneous thinking among 21st-century attitudes. This is the most direct, Biblical, well-organized, and presented treatise I have ever read that disarms the demonic poverty spirit. Many writings in the area of finances are self-serving and non-biblical. Dr. Blair's work is saturated in scripture and has been proven in his own life.

His grasp of the scriptures includes clear use of the ancient Hebrew words that clarify God's promises to supply His servants!

Finally, this book is just a pleasure to read! Well outlined, it moves to a powerful conclusion. For those who teach and preach, it is a wealth of inspired truth! Dr. Blair's gifted ministry of equipping believers flows through this Spirit-anointed work. I commend this powerful book with all my heart.

Dr. Ron Phillips
Pastor Emeritus Abba's House
Chattanooga, Tennessee

Introduction

Warning: This book is hazardous to your poverty and areas of lack. I may come off bold and firm in this book, but I promise you that if you can conquer any offense the verbiage or wording may cause, you will see God move in your life like you never have before. This book will teach you concepts that traditional church people may take issue with, but what you're about to read is proven to work. Not only are they proven to work, but they're biblical as well.

I have discovered that most people struggle in two main areas of their lives: their health and wealth. This book is designed to forge in you the consciousness of wealth. You will discover how God and wealth are connected. Being poor doesn't make you more godly.

Church people need to repent from poverty! If this statement offends you, then you're not ready for the contents of this book. If you're one of those who think that we don't need to talk about money but preach the gospel, then you're part of the problem. It takes money to preach the gospel. As I always say, "go ye is going to cost ye."

Missions cost money. That's why most missionaries ask for donations. Even if you're the evangelist who preaches on the street corner, money aided in that. The gas you needed to get to the street corner, the clothes you had on the day you preached on the corner, the bullhorn, microphone, speaker, tracts, or whatever tools you used to help you evangelize costs money. Without money, you can't do ministry effectively. Honestly, it's hard to do any good for anyone without money.

How can you help a person when both of you are living in the same conditions? Just as a drug addict cannot help other drug addicts come off drugs, a poor man cannot help poor men come out of poverty. When it comes to wealth, you must transcend a person's economic status to help them. Money is a tool to better the lives of people. If you do not want to help people, you're just selfish and self-righteous.

This book teaches you how to agree with God concerning your wealth. Haven't you noticed that those that are the wealthiest tend to do the most good for people? I'm not talking about a few bad examples; I'm speaking about overall. It's time to get delivered from poverty and lack so that you can come into the abundance God has for you. This is part of God's will and covenant for you.

To deny this is to deny the gospel itself. I will prove to you later that prosperity comes with the gospel of salvation. So let us dive into this revelation and conquer the limiting beliefs that keep us in lack and dysfunctional cycles.

1

Sign Of The Covenant

When God raised certain people up throughout the Bible, they also became wealthy. Every prominent figure in scripture that God used for His glory became rich. See, we have not been taught that wealth comes with God. As a result, we demonize the rich and honor poverty, making it almost shameful to have a lot of money and possessions.

This is the mindset of the vast majority of the church. Then when someone like myself or the many others that had come before me and paved the way comes along, you label us as heretics. Our message is labeled as the "prosperity gospel." I'm sure I will get some kickback for even writing this book, but I only teach and endorse what works. Did you know that prosperity is part of the gospel? I will prove this to you a little later on.

POWER TO GET WEALTH

"But thou shalt remember the LORD thy God: for it is he that giveth thee power to get wealth, that he may establish his covenant which he sware unto thy fathers, as it is this day." Deuteronomy 8:18

God gives us the power to get wealth. Power in Hebrew is the word *"kōaḥ"* (ko'-akh) which means strength, power, might, and ability to accomplish a thing. So what God is saying here is that proof of His covenant with us is in our God-given strength and ability to get wealth. When you're in covenant with God, curses are broken, thus making prosperity obtainable.

Listen, I struggled financially my entire adult life. I didn't come into some huge inheritance, nor did I have someone to mentor me concerning financial success until later on. And yet, I'm living the best life I have ever had. Why is this? Because I got a revelation and a personal conviction concerning the covenant promises and provisions of God.

I began studying and understanding the power He gave me to get wealth, and I started from scratch too. It doesn't matter what kind of background or past you have. I'm a high school dropout, and here it is I have broken generational curses of poverty and all other kinds of dysfunction. It wasn't until I developed the right mindset and attitude towards wealth that I began to see a major change in my life. When I discovered God's ability in me to produce the reality I wanted, my life began to change drastically.

Remember, God has given you the power to get wealth. This means that your prosperity is your responsibility. Many of us are too busy putting it on God when He already put it in us. Maybe this is why your prayers of provision are not being answered. You keep looking up when you should be looking within.

Some may say, "well brother, that sounds like new age teaching to me." My response to such people would be, "well, it seems to me that the new agers have a better understanding of God's provision than most professed Christians." Church folks give everything to the devil and then wonder why he prospers in what he does. God has given us the ability to make our own way prosperous. You don't have to wonder whether or not it's God's will for you to prosper.

Why would God give you the power or ability to prosper if He didn't desire for you to prosper? Don't let church brain make you dumb. We have to think on these things to get the results we want.

"This book of the law shall not depart out of thy mouth; but thou shalt meditate therein day and night, that thou mayest observe to do according to all that is written therein: for then thou shalt make thy way prosperous, and then thou shalt have good success." Joshua 1:8

Again, we can clearly see that our prosperity is our responsibility. God has given us everything we need to prosper. God told Joshua not to let the law book depart from his mouth. In other words, your confessions, decrees, and proclamation are vital to your prosperity.

"Death and life *are* in the power of the tongue: and they that love it shall eat the fruit thereof." Proverbs 18:21

We see the word power again in this verse. But this time, the Hebrew word for power is *"yād"* (yawd) which means hand. So your speech has the creative power to direct your life for the desired outcome.

"Behold, we put bits in the horses' mouths, that they may obey us; and we turn about their whole body. Behold also the ships, which though they be so great, and are driven of fierce winds, yet are they turned about with a very small helm, whithersoever the governor listeth." James 3:3,4

This scripture speaks about the power of the tongue. You steer a horse by the bit in its mouth. You steer a ship but the rudder underneath. Your words shape your world. Conversations become manifestations. In your tongue is the power to get wealth!

If you want God-like results, you must speak in alignment with what God agrees with. The tongue is one of the smallest members of your body, yet it is one of the most powerful tools God has given you to produce the results of God's covenant with you. You must understand the power that worketh in you. Now let us look at what else God told Joshua.

God also told Joshua to meditate day and night. God commanded Joshua to meditate on the very laws he was confessing out of his mouth. Your mouth and mind must align with God's covenant provision for you to make your way prosperous. Meditate in Hebrew is the word *"hāgâ"* (haw-gaw') which means to utter, devise, plot, ponder, and imagine. So meditation has everything to do with thinking upon a thing and repeating it back to yourself.

It's like reading out loud everything your mind is imagining. Biblical meditation is the focus of thought and self-talk. Scripture teaches us that out of the abundance of the heart, the mouth will speak (Matthew 12:34). Whatever your heart is full of will eventually come out in what you say. What rules your heart will rule your mouth. What rules your mouth will rule your life. This is why you have to have the right things in you.

Do you now see the power that God has given you? People in other religions and those with different beliefs surely understand this. These are some of the very things they teach and practice in secular business seminars. These are habits of the wealthy, which is why they become successful. God has given equal opportunity for success to everyone, regardless of their belief or lifestyle of choice.

WEALTH COMES WITH GOD

All men have the ability to get wealth. Suppose this is indeed the case; how much more are those who serve God? It's time that we stop separating God from money and possessions. I find that many Christians criticize the wealthy but can't measure up to their stature and influence. It's foolish to criticize those that are of your league.

The men of God in scripture who served God were wealthy men. God blesses those who serve Him and walk with Him even more than those who benefit from His resources and blessing. Look at what the scriptures say about Abraham.

"And Abram *was* very rich in cattle, in silver, and in gold." Genesis 13:2

Abraham wasn't just rich; he was very rich. This man is the father of our faith, according to scripture. So that means that we are to follow his example of faith towards God. It seems to me that faith in God made Abraham a very rich man. Though Abraham didn't appear to be materialistic, that didn't stop him from acquiring such things.

The father of our faith was rich with possessions and money. If he is our example of faith, then how rich are we supposed to be that follow his example? Even though I'm speaking specifically about Abraham, study everyone that God used significantly in scripture. Everyone who walked closely with God was wealthy. They had precious metals and a lot of possessions.

It's the will of God for you to have more. God is a God of more than enough. Abraham was a man who had a relationship with God, and with that relationship came an abundance of provision. It's almost considered heresy to connect God with wealth, but this was the reality that

Abraham lived in. As the father of our faith, we should experience the same reality of wealth he experienced.

Our faith in God should produce wealth. Everyone who walked with God was wealthy. And even if they had a season where they lacked, God used someone to provide. So those who walk with God should have access to an abundant supply of provision. Faith gives you the right to become rich.

What you do with your riches determines the deity you serve. See, money isn't the issue. It's the altar where you have chosen to give your money that can be the problem. Money is a tool you use to build whatever kingdom you are a part of and worship whatever God that may be ruling your heart. Don't you see that money isn't the problem? If there is a problem, money will reveal it.

If you are a sincere believer in God, you should be prospering. You should have enough money to live comfortably and do the will of God. We can't compare the poverty of those before us to our day and age. Resources are more available now than ever before. If the men and women of God that we read about in scripture defeated poverty, then that should be a standard example for you and I.

Also, let us examine Noah. The ark he built was vast and spacious. You not only had to have supernatural help to build it, but I'm also sure it took an abundance of land and resources. A poor man with a poor family could not have built such a massive structure. It takes riches to build for God! This is why we need to change our minds and attitude toward wealth.

God has not designed for you to live in defeat. Though you have a humble beginning, God desires you to have an epic finish. When you are in covenant with God, and you appropriate the benefits of that covenant, wealth comes by standard and birthright. Everyone that was in covenant with God in scripture was wealthy. As beneficiaries of the new covenant, we are to be recipients of wealth and riches as well.

PREACH THE GOSPEL TO THE POOR

"The Spirit of the Lord is upon me, because he hath anointed me to preach the gospel to the poor..." Luke 4:18

This is the part of Jesus' ministry that's not highlighted enough. Whenever I hear people preach against the prosperity message, they love to say that we need to get back to preaching the gospel and winning souls. But according to the scripture we just read, the gospel was first to be preached to the poor. Since the gospel is the good news, what good news could you possibly give to a poor person?

The good news to poor people is that they no longer have to be poor. Not only can they be lifted out of their poverty, but they can also be introduced to a system and level of consciousness that will make them rich and keep them rich. See, Jesus preached repentance along with the message of the kingdom. Repent means to change your mind or to think differently afterward. To access the wealth and riches of the kingdom of God in the earth, you must repent (change your mind) and be converted to God's way.

"Beloved, I wish above all things that thou mayest prosper and be in health, even as thy soul prospereth." 3 John 1:2

You will never prosper in life until you prosper in your soul. The gospel of the kingdom comes to deliver your soul from poverty. If it keeps you in poverty, then it is not the gospel! If it does not address and rewire the parts of your thinking that keep you in cycles of poverty, then it's not the gospel! Prosperity is an inter-covenant promise.

From the Old Testament to the new testament, we see the promises for prosperity transcending earthly covenants. It's a promise throughout all generations of the earth. When you understand this, you can prosper and thrive in any economy. I believe Jesus laid out the priority of the gospel. He preached the gospel to the poor; then he healed the brokenhearted, then He preached deliverance to the captives, then He recovered sight to the blind, and then He liberated those that were bruised.

Jesus listed preaching prosperity before He listed preaching deliverance or healing. You can't preach the kingdom or any new covenant theology concept without preaching prosperity also. Prosperity is a part of any covenant God makes, and it's no different in the new covenant. So let us repent for being poor and renew our minds to agree with the unlimited supply of God. Prosperity is a major part of the gospel.

2

Jesus Standard For Wealth

Some tend to think that wealthy people are not humble or that wealthy people won't choose a more humble path. Well, you don't get any more humble than the Lord Jesus Christ. Jesus had a humility even greater than what Moses had. As the supreme ruler of the universe under God the Father, Jesus took on the form of a servant.

"Who, being in the form of God, tho ught it not robbery to be equal with God: But made himself of no reputation, and took upon him the form of a servant, and was made in the likeness of men: And being found in fashion as a man, he humbled himself, and became obedient unto death, even the death of the cross. Wherefore God also hath highly exalted him, and given him a name which is above every name" Philippians 2:6-9

When one leaves their lofty estate to take a lesser form and live a lesser life just to lay down that life, there's no greater love and humility than that. So we can conclude that Jesus is the most humble man in existence. But even in His lowly state, he still lived life by a certain standard. Some say that Jesus was poor, but that is not consistent with scripture. Just because He lived a humble life doesn't mean He was poor.

JESUS WAS NOT POOR

"For ye know the grace of our Lord Jesus Christ, that, though he was rich, yet for your sakes he became poor, that ye through his poverty might be rich." 2 Corinthians 8:9

People use this scripture as a reference for Jesus' earthly ministry, stating that He was just a little pitiful poor man doing the will of the Father. Such people suggest that Jesus was poor during His earthly ministry. But as we will soon find out, Jesus was very rich! But before we go there, I want to highlight when did Jesus actually become poor. As we will see, Jesus was not poor during His earthly ministry.

So when did Jesus become poor? Jesus became poor on the cross. When his high-quality garments were stripped from him, and He hung on the cross naked for all to see, that was the ultimate sign of disgrace and humiliation. In essence, Jesus was stripped of royalty at that moment and reduced to poverty, all while bearing the other sins and sicknesses of the world in His body. The only time Jesus was poor was when He was on the cross.

Obviously, He wasn't poor during His earthly ministry. Let us look at the riches Jesus Possessed.

- **Jesus was wealthy at birth:** "And when they were come into the house, they saw the young child with Mary his mother, and fell down, and worshipped him: and when they had opened their treasures, they presented unto him gifts; gold, and frankincense and myrrh" Matthew 2:11 KJV

When the magi and wisemen visited Jesus, they presented very expensive gifts to Him. Gold, frankincense, and myrrh were very costly back then and are costly until now. Jesus was set for life from the time He was born. There was no day on earth that Jesus experienced poverty except when He was crucified on the cross. All of this Jesus experienced as an infant.

If our Lord and Savior were rich as an infant, what are you supposed to be as a believer? Many non-believers understand this, and this is why unbelievers tend to be wiser than believers. Some may even say that you need to mature more in Christ before getting wealth, but here it is, Jesus was already wealthy from the day He was born. Maturity is seen in how you handle wealth; it does not dictate whether or not you deserve it. So even if you're newly born again as a believer, you still have the power to get wealth.

- **Jesus owned much property and goods:** "And

Joanna the wife of Chuza Herod's steward, and Susanna, and many others, which ministered unto him of their substance." Luke 8:3

The word substance in Greek literally means property, possessions, and goods. This tells me that Jesus had more wealth, possessions, and property than what scripture mentions, and this leaves room for us only to imagine how much Jesus actually had during His life on earth. Want to talk about materialism? Jesus had a lot of it.

- Jesus had a treasurer (accountant): "For some *of them* thought, because Judas had the bag, that Jesus had said unto him, Buy *those things* that we have need of against the feast; or, that he should give something to the poor" John 13:29

Only rich people need a treasurer or accountant. When you have more money than you can manage, you need someone to help you manage it. Also, Jesus took responsibility for His team even though they had their own wealth. We see this in the fact that Jesus paid His and Peter's taxes as well (Matthew 17:24-27). Jesus had so much money that His thieving treasurer didn't put a dent in their profits.

"And Jesus sat over against the treasury, and beheld how the people cast money into the treasury: and many that were rich cast in much." Mark 12:41

It was customary for people to give to Jesus' treasury.

This was the same treasury that Judas was responsible for managing. This was a major part of the apostles' income, the people's giving into the treasury. Think about that next time you tell your pastor they need to get a regular job.

- Jesus wore quality clothing: "Then the soldiers, when they had crucified Jesus, took his garments, and made four parts, to every soldier a part; and also his coat: now the coat was without seam, woven from the top throughout. They said therefore among themselves, Let us not rend it, but cast lots for it, whose it shall be: that the scripture might be fulfilled, which saith, They parted my raiment among them, and for my vesture they did cast lots. These things therefore the soldiers did" John 19:23,24 KJV

At the site of the crucifixion of Jesus, Roman soldiers gambled for His garments. You don't gamble for things that are of low quality. What Jesus had on was of high-value material. If Jesus was as poor as many people teach, why would Roman soldiers gamble for His clothes at the cross? This tells us that Jesus had high-quality taste in clothing.

If Jesus were walking the earth today, He would probably be wearing Gucci or Dolce and Gabanna. We have to change our minds about Jesus and what we think He is like. It's not necessarily about being flashy; it's just part of who He is as a person. Most religious people would be offended by Jesus' modern fashion if He walked the

IT'S GODLY TO BE RICH 15

earth today. The fact that His clothes were gambled for should tell us that Jesus had good taste in quality clothing. There's nothing wrong with dressing nice.

- **Jesus owned a house:** "And it came to pass, that, as Jesus sat at meat in his house, many publicans and sinners sat also together with Jesus and his disciples: for there were many, and they followed him" Matthew 2:15 KJV

Poor men don't own houses! For all the religious people who say they want to be like Jesus, why are you still renting if He owned a home? I'm not condemning those renting; however, you should aim to have more in life. This is especially because Jesus had more in life, and if He had more in life, you should want more for yourself. As the text shows, Jesus was hospitable to those who came to His house.

It's hard to be hospitable to people in a tiny house. I'm sure Jesus' house had enough room to accommodate all the religious leaders who ate with Him and His disciples. Even though Jesus traveled a lot during His earthly ministry, He still had a home that was His that He could come back to. God's will is for all of His people to own a home. Renting is not your portion!

- **Jesus distinguished Himself from the poor:** "For the poor always ye have with you; but me ye have not always." John 12:8 KJV

Some people may think it's arrogant to distinguish yourself from the poor. But you can't help the poor if you identify with their current poverty status. You can't help the poor when you're poor too. Jesus made sure that He didn't lump Himself into the category of the poor. Though He ministered to the poor, Jesus also ensured He couldn't be categorized as poor. Now, this is no reason to look down on the poor.

Scripture has many blessings and promises for remembering and blessing poor people. But that doesn't mean you have to become poor to bless the poor. If you want to be rich in life, you must learn to have mercy on the poor, but at the same time, you must distinguish yourself from the poor. Notice that Jesus fed the poor and ministered to them, but He didn't hang around them. You will never prosper hanging around the very thing crippling you.

THE DISCIPLES JESUS CHOSE

Let us examine the disciples that Jesus chose. I want you to notice that He did not pick poor men to train in the ministry with him. Jesus picked men with wealthy backgrounds and lucrative trades and chose men who knew how to make money and get things done. If God hated riches and wealth so much, why did Jesus pick rich men to be His disciples and lead His church? We have to stop being silly and listening to poor-minded people.

Andrew, Peter, James, and John were all fishermen (Matthew 4:18-22). Based upon John 21:2-8, it's said that Thomas, Nathaniel, and Phillip were fishermen as well.

Being a fisherman during biblical times was a lucrative trade; everyone ate fish. We also know Matthew was a tax collector (Matthew 9: 9,10; 10:3). Simon was known as a zealot (Matthew 10:4).

A zealot was known as one who engaged in politics. They were known to be radical in wanting to overthrow the Roman government. So Simon was most likely a political revolutionary. I'm pretty sure he wasn't poor either. As we see in today's political climate, it takes money to move a campaign forward, and the more people believe in you, the more you are funded by those people.

Scripture doesn't specifically say what the rest of the disciples did, but from the apparent choices He made, Jesus did not pick poor unproductive men to lead His church. It's not just about the wealth, but it's about what the wealth communicates. Money reveals your heart, and money reveals your wisdom. God will not leave the church and the kingdom in the hands of those who are not competent. Jesus chose those to be on His team that had similar business acumen.

Though God loves all people, He only employs the wise and productive to be high officials. If He can't find any in the church, He will employ those outside of the church to get things done on the earth that He wants. So while Christians claim that they don't listen to "worldly people," God has chosen many of them to accomplish specific tasks in the earth to advance His kingdom. This is why scripture says the children of the world are wiser than the children of light (Luke 16:18). And Jesus was talking in the context of money here.

God will always choose the wise to lead first. Why do you think Jesus chose Paul to be one of the top apostles of his generation? Not because Paul was a good man but because he was wise and skilled. Besides being a chief Pharisee, Paul also had tent-making skills. According to Jewish scholars, tent-making wasn't about actual tents but about tallits or what we call prayer shawls today.

The apostle Paul was a tallit maker, a very lucrative trade back them. All Jews were commanded to have one, so you know that was a job always in demand. So outside of Paul being a religious zealot before his conversion to Christ, he was also a skilled businessman who knew how to make money. Jesus never chose poor people to lead His church. Just because they didn't always flash it doesn't mean they didn't have it.

I hear many stories about how men of God came into the ministry struggling for resources and provision, having to scratch and claw their way to get to the top. This is not God's way. A thorough study of scripture will prove that the people God used to do great things from the old testament to the new testament were not poor doing the work of God, and they started off wealthy. You're not supposed to start ministry being poor. You should never have to choose between paying your bills and paying the church's bills.

Though it may seem noble, it's actually a violation of kingdom protocol for how God raises senior leadership. If Jesus didn't start His ministry in financial struggle, then why are you? You are never supposed to start a ministry or church in lack! David wanted to build God a house, but God told him that his son Solomon would build God a house. Before God allowed Solomon to finish building Him a house, God caused Solomon to complete the building of his own house (1 Kings 7).

Could it be that some of you are struggling in ministry because you failed to build your house first? Why would God have you build what you can't maintain? If you can't manage your own house, then you can't manage the house of God. Notice in 1 Timothy 3 that senior leadership qualification is all natural. It has nothing to do with your anointing; it has everything to do with your character and wise management of your home.

I understand stepping out on faith, but you should not be trying to start a ministry if you're poor. Jesus didn't do it, the disciples didn't do it, and Paul didn't do it either. Jesus told His apostles not to bring any gold, silver, brass, money bags, or extra articles of clothing for their ministry journey (Matthew 10:9,10). He said that the workman is worthy of his meat. In other words, don't bring or use your personal wealth for ministry.

Let the people you minister to compensate you. Why would Jesus tell them not to bring something they didn't have? The apostles were rich before ministry, but Jesus wanted the ministry to provide for itself. This is why you're out of order when you are constantly putting up your personal money for ministry. If you're the senior leader, you shouldn't be coming out of your pocket to pay the church's bills.

Jesus built a following and a movement before He started a church. He was not only a trained rabbi but also a skilled carpenter, which was another lucrative trade during that time. So while Jesus prepared for ministry, He also had a skill that made Him money. If you're called to full-time ministry, you also need to learn another craft or trade that can make you some money. In the times we live in now, there's no excuse.

There are teenagers becoming multi-millionaires but using their phones and tablets. It's easier to become rich today than in previous generations. People are learning to trade, and it's making them rich. I would dare say that you should get into financial services before fully entering the ministry. Then you'll have something to bring your followers into as well. If Jesus was wealthy before He fully began His ministry, you and I should follow that same model.

If you really want to be like Jesus, get wealthy like Jesus. He has a standard of wealth that all of us should follow. Wealth is proof of wisdom and productivity, and these are the kind of people God employs to work for Him.

3

Distinguished From Poverty

As we can see so far, Jesus was not a poor man as many misinformed ministers teach. Not only was Jesus rich, but He chose other rich men to aid in leading His movement and His church. If this offends you, then you are the problem here. To disagree with having riches is to disagree with God. There needs to be national repentance among church people for shunning abundance and embracing poverty.

What can you really expect to accomplish being poor and lacking resources? It's the people with the most money that rules the world. Wealth gives you influence, and you can't change anything without influence. The wealthy only listen to their own, and if the wealthy rule the world, your reach will be very limited while trying to change things. I'm talking to religious people here.

Look at some of the wealthier churches in a region. They are the ones who seem to have the greatest religious voice and representation. I've never heard of or seen a governor or president visit a storefront church or a church with limited seating capacity. I'm not putting down small churches; I'm just speaking a fact here. Wealth speaks, and wealth attracts its own.

You have to be wealthy to attract more people who are wealthy. You have to possess some kind of influence to attract others who are influential. This is how things are and how things work. Yes, God can and does give favor, but at the same time, favor is supposed to establish you in this reality. I had seen favor run dry in many lives because they didn't steward it properly when God was blessing them.

This is why we must learn to be distinguished from poverty. I believe this is the secret to Jesus' prosperity, and this is the secret to a thriving body of believers.

NEVER IDENTIFY WITH POVERTY

"There came unto him a woman having an alabaster box of very precious ointment, and poured it on his head, as he sat at meat. But when his disciples saw it, they had indignation, saying, To what purpose is this waste? For this ointment might have been sold for much, and given to the poor. When Jesus understood it, he said unto them, Why trouble ye the woman? for she hath wrought a good work upon me. For ye have the poor always with you; but me ye have not always." Matthew 26:7-11

Notice that the disciples were upset that Jesus had expensive oil poured over his feet. They started saying how this expensive oil could have been sold, and the money could have been given to the poor. Jesus rebuked them for speaking against what she did to Him, calling it a good work. Listen, you can't do good works without money. It takes money to do something good for God.

Money provides the ability to present something in excellence. What this woman did to Jesus was done in excellence. The oil was costly, but she saw that Jesus was worthy of the expense and more. One thing we don't realize about Jesus that's outlined in scripture is that He was a regular recipient of precious gifts. There were women who followed His ministry that gave to Him often (Luke 8:3).

Today we get offended when men and women of God are presented with nice things regularly. Here it is, Jesus was accustomed to such treatment, and at that moment, His own disciples were His haters. It's silly to assume that because people wear expensive clothes, live in a big house, or drive a luxury vehicle, they're not giving to the poor. Only poor-minded people try to regulate how the rich spend their money. Instead of learning, they'd rather criticize.

But Jesus said something very interesting after His disciples criticized the woman for "wasting" her ointment on Him. Jesus said in verse 11, "For ye have the poor always with you; but me ye have not always." In other words, there will always be poor people for you to give to. Notice that Jesus distinguished Himself from the poor as well. Though He did not look down on them, Jesus was careful not to categorize Himself with them.

You can't help the poor as long as you're in the same class as them. For Jesus to preach the gospel to the poor, He first had to be rich to qualify. Otherwise, He would have been a hypocrite. Jesus fed the poor and preached the gospel to the poor, but He never identified Himself as poor. Notice also that Jesus ministered to the poor, but He never hung around them.

If He did hang around anyone outside of His disciples, it was rich sinners. Think about that! Even when it came to His lodging, when He did stay in someone's house, it was in the house of someone wealthy. Jesus loved every one, but He had a personal standard for Himself. Just because others are poor doesn't mean that you reduce yourself to poverty.

There will always be poor people to minister to and feed, but your prosperity must be consistently fed to be sustained. The more you have, the more will be given. This is a universal law! Jesus' ability to help the poor was because He wasn't one of them. You must have it in order to give it. This is why you need to be wealthy!

THE RICH RULE

You need wealth so that you can provide and rule. We cannot rule in this life without money. There are only two categories you can fit in, and the bible outlines them clearly. Either you're the head or the tail, above or beneath, lender or borrower, blessed or cursed, and rich or poor. Society may have in-between to make everyone feel better about almost getting there. But scripturally, there is no in-between or a "middle class."

"The rich ruleth over the poor, and the borrower *is* servant to the lender." Proverbs 22:7

The rich are the ones that are ruling. There's no getting around this. Having money positions you to have influence, and it can bring you into spaces and among people that everyone can't get to. You can't rule without riches. Many may say, "well, money is not everything." Money may not be everything, but according to scripture, it's the answer to everything (Ecclesiastes 10:19).

Most of the problems we have in this nation and others are that we don't have the right people in positions of rulership. Things would be better if we had the right people in rulership. But I've also discovered that the right people are not funded. And those with the right intentions that are funded have to bend to the will of the donors. Righteous rulers will require righteous donors.

Do you want to change the political landscape of our nation? Get some money and support the right candidate that agrees with God. If the righteous are not in authority, they don't have the right backing and the right funding. The ones who have the money are the ones who make the rules.

"When the righteous are in authority, the people rejoice: but when the wicked beareth rule, the people mourn." Proverbs 29:2

This is true in other societal systems, not just politics. If you want to rule in that realm, you must have the money to do so. There's an old saying that you must pay the cost to be the boss—those with the most money rule in their sphere. I hear church people constantly complain about people in high places while watching them and never aspiring to be there themselves. All the while, the non-church people are doing more than the church.

You can't complain against something you're not trying to outmatch. This is something I try to tell my fellow African Americans. Our voice will never make a difference until our money starts making a difference. Do you want to know what's more important than your march? Your money!

We need to learn from what happened at black wall street to fortify and multiply our wealth. Just like some currencies are backed by gold, we need voices backed by wealth. There need to be more righteous people in place to stop the injustices in our nation. Systemic racism is becoming a thing of the past. There are more black millionaires and billionaires now than ever.

If black people want to see change, we must unite and put our dollars behind our voices. Let your money be your defense (Ecclesiastes 7:12). Riches position you for rulership; you can't rule if you're not rich. How can you help the less fortunate or the oppressed if you're not ruling anything? I have discovered that those with the most complaints do the very least to improve the situation. Don't complain about being oppressed when there are plenty of opportunities out there for you to come from under that yoke.

I look at people who stay in the hood their entire life, and all I hear is excuses about your environment when there are plenty of examples of those who left the hood and made it. But many would rather keep an image than be looked at as a square or someone who's not loyal to the hood. If you want to make it out of a bad environment, you must disengage from the mentality that kept you in there. To better yourself, you must reach out to where better is. This may be in the form of reading books or reaching out for mentorship.

However it looks for you initially, you must pursue where you are trying to go. And I promise you that the law of attraction is real. If you can see yourself out of a bad situation and pursue steps towards that, then you will magnetize opportunities your way to make that happen. This is the basics of how faith works. To learn more about this, read my book, The Science Of Faith.

Whatever situation you're in, you must start preparing yourself to rule over that which is ruling over you. You do this by first doing what Jesus did by distinguishing yourself from your environment. This work of repentance starts in the soul first. You can't rule in life until you first establish God's rule of prosperity in your heart, for whatever rules your heart will rule your life. This is why scripture is clear when it says as a man thinks in his heart, that's what he becomes (Proverbs 23:7).

To be distinguished from poverty, you must come out of agreement with it in your soul. As prosperity begins to rule your life, you will start to rule in life. Consciousness is creative in nature. The mind shapes your life's experiences. Being that He was around wealth all His life, Jesus was able to distinguish Himself from the poor, which positioned Him to help the poor properly.

Though He never identified with the poor, He never looked down on them. There are quite a few blessings outlined in scripture for blessing the poor. Those who are more fortunate have a duty to bless the less fortunate. But you must be blessed to be a blessing, and you can't bless the poor if you are poor also. It's time to think and do differently in this regard.

How you treat those less fortunate than you will determine how God treats you. But in the midst of this, you must not lose your status. You don't have to become poor to reach the poor; I have seen some religiously attempt this. Even those such as Roman Catholic priests take vows of poverty. I remember seeing a priest be penalized for driving a luxury car.

But one thing about that car was that it got the attention of young men in the neighborhood. These were probably the same young men he wanted to reach. This is an example of how wealth can be used as a tool of evangelism. I remember the Lord speaking to me something I had never heard before one day. Sometime last year, the Lord said to me that entrepreneurship would be the next form of evangelism.

I know that messes with your religion, but that's what He said to me. This means that God will use money, assets, resources, aid, business, and such like things to reveal Christ and draw people to Him. Money will be a major factor in bringing people to Christ in this generation and the one to come. Some people, you will not win to Christ unless you can deliver them out of their situation. And there are others who will never hear you unless you're greater than them economically.

Preaching on the street corners won't do much in this day and age unless you have some miracles or a better life to present to people. People need hope, and money is the answer. Some of you may say, "no, Jesus is the answer." While He may be the answer, resources and provision come with Him. So you can't have all of Jesus without having provision as well.

It will be very hard to win and keep the lost without power and prosperity. So while some of you are preaching about winning souls, you need to make sure you got something in your life they can be inspired by as well. Prosperity is more important than you think, and no one wants to accept Jesus in their life to end up living a life of financial struggle. Yes, your faith will cause you to lay down your life, but you should gain a better one in the process that is full of love, faith, and riches.

4

Ownership and Possessions

Now that we have established that Jesus was rich, the apostles were rich, and just about every prominent figure God used in scripture was rich, we will now explore what riches afford us to have. I proved to you already that Jesus was a man of great possessions. He had a house, a lot of money, and possessions or assets that scripture doesn't specifically mention. So if it's good enough for Jesus, it should be good enough for us. There's nothing wrong with having an abundance of nice things.

We love to quote that God is the God of more than enough. Somehow, we seem only to believe that when it comes to others, but the same is true for you. God wants you to have more than enough of everything, and this includes houses, vehicles, businesses, and anything of substance. We have to get rid of our fear of more. Religion makes you feel guilty for wanting more when God is the God of more than enough.

There needs to be nationwide repentance from poverty in American churches. We believe in beautifying the church but not our homes. This has to stop, and it must stop with you!

IT'S TIME TO UPGRADE YOUR LIVING

"In my Father's house are many mansions: if it were not so, I would have told you. I go to prepare a place for you." John 14:2

Some translations replace mansions with rooms. But either way you look at it, it still describes the abundance of supply and quality of living in God's world. I come to tell you that there are mansions in heaven, and the rooms in God's personal house are probably the size of mansions. If there are mansions and large rooms in heaven, then why not have that on earth as well? Many of us want to preach thy kingdom come until it's time to talk about wealth.

Thy kingdom come means that what's in God's world is now invading ours. This is not just in the area of miracles and the supernatural but also in the area of wealth, possessions, and innovation. God doesn't just want you to be healed; God also wants you to be rich. Owning a nice house or a mansion should be a goal of yours. If we are going to be like Jesus, we need to be like Him in all things, including riches.

"...and hast built goodly houses, and dwelt therein"
Deuteronomy 8:12

God desires for you to dwell in goodly houses. Goodly
in Hebrew is *"ṭôḇ"* (tobe), which means good, pleasant,
agreeable, benefit, and welfare. God told Israel to
remember Him and His commandments after they
inherited the land and built their goodly houses. Part of
God's promise for you is a higher quality of living. Notice
that land and houses were part of God's promise to Israel.

This is why we should want to own land and houses
today. Have you ever sat back and wondered why real
estate was so important to God? He wanted His people
to conquer land and build Him a house. This is why you
should want land and houses as well.

"And it shall be, when the Lord thy God shall have
brought thee into the land which he sware unto thy
fathers, to Abraham, to Isaac, and to Jacob, to give thee
great and goodly cities, which thou buildedst not, And
houses full of all good things, which thou filledst not, and
wells digged, which thou diggedst not, vineyards and olive
trees, which thou plantedst not; when thou shalt have
eaten and be full; Then beware lest thou forget the Lord,
which brought thee forth out of the land of Egypt, from
the house of bondage." Deuteronomy 6:10-12

God wants us to have and live in goodly cities. He
doesn't want you living in the ghetto. One day, I heard a
man of God say, "God wants you to go from the ghetto to
the get mo (slang for more)." He wants you to have wells,
vineyards, and olive trees. In other words, God wants to

have appreciating assets that you can profit from and eat from. See, God doesn't have an issue with us being wealthy; he only has an issue when we forsake Him because of the wealth.

"Take ye the spoil of silver, take the spoil of gold: for there is none end of the store and glory out of all the pleasant furniture." Nahum 2:9

What if I told you that God wants you to have nice furniture? God wants you to take your spoil of silver, gold, and pleasant furniture. What do you think the furniture in heaven is like? Your stuff should be of similar quality on the earth. You may not be there right now, but it should be your goal.

Have you ever wondered why you always felt like you were supposed to do more, be more, and have more in life? Something in you is never satisfied until you're able to have that lifestyle. This is because it's part of who God is. Look at all of the riches Israel had and all the riches they were promised. Our Heavenly Father doesn't have an issue with His people prospering. He wants to be included in the profit.

THE FLAMBOYANCE OF GOD

Another thing I discovered about God is that He's very flashy. That's right, you are reading it correctly. God is flashy and flamboyant. You may be saying to yourself, how so? Let us go to the scriptures to prove this.

"In the year that king Uzziah died I saw also the Lord

sitting upon a throne, high and lifted up, and his train filled the temple. Above it stood the seraphims: each one had six wings; with twain he covered his face, and with twain he covered his feet, and with twain he did fly. And one cried unto another, and said, Holy, holy, holy, is the Lord of hosts: the whole earth is full of his glory. And the posts of the door moved at the voice of him that cried, and the house was filled with smoke." Isaiah 6:1-4

What I'm about to teach you in this moment is what the Lord revealed to me about the glory of God that many people overlook. Isaiah saw the Lord sitting on His throne in this encounter with God, high and lifted up. The train of His robe filled the temple. If that isn't flashy and loud, I don't know what is. It's impossible not to notice God because it's in His character to be seen. Scripture describes 24 elders with crowns on their heads seated around God's throne.

It also describes lightning, thunder, a sea of glass, heavenly creatures, worship, and honor around His throne (Revelation 4:5-11). All of these things are noticeable, loud, and flashy. The Seraphim were declaring the glory of the Lord around God's throne. Glory in Hebrew is the word "*kābôd*" (kaw-bode') Which means honor, splendor, and abundance. There is no glory without wealth!

So with all of the splendor of God's throne and personhood, God is also wealthy and flashy. His throne is noticeable, His servants are loud, His robe is noticeable, and the way He is honored is noticeable. Everything about God is flashy and noticeable. The glory of God is noticeable. So with all of the precious promises of provision that we have, God wants it to be noticeable in our lives.

God wants your houses, furniture, vehicles, clothing, and even your life to be noticeable. Everything the Lord desires for you, He wants it to be grand. When the glory of God is on your life, almost everything about you becomes noticeable. Jesus said we are to be the light of the world and a city upon a hill that cannot be hidden (Matthew 5:14). What if I told you that God wants you to be flashy?

I'm not speaking of being flashy in arrogance, but flashy in righteousness (right standing). When you are right with God, His resources should be right with you. Even as God is to be seen and noticed in heaven, God wants to be seen or recognized in every area of your life. Your wealth is included in this. Let your light (the light of His glory) shine in your life.

God wants His light to be seen. Darkness is what keeps things hidden. It's not the will of God for you to hide your wealth. God doesn't want the wealth to corrupt your character. We have been convinced by persecutors of prosperity that hiding our wealth is humility.

And yet heaven is full of beauty and splendor to be seen before all who partake of its goodness. God doesn't have the same hang-ups that we have. Wealth and riches are standard living Him. God is so used to having it that He's not moved or corrupted by it. See, we need to get used to having money and valuables for an extended time. Most mature people who have been wealthy for years are not moved by wealth.

We must get used to having money and having possessions as a usual standard of life. I have found that those who are not used to having money become prideful baby tyrants when they get it. This is why your consciousness must be shaped to agree with wealth and handle wealth. Did you know that everything we have on earth that God has in excess? If He's the God of more than enough, then surely He's the first partaker of this nature in and of Himself.

There is an excess of things we value on earth, even in the cosmos. Did you know that it rains diamonds on the planets Saturn and Jupiter? And yet diamonds are mined in Russia, Africa, and Australia, among other places. Diamonds symbolize wealth because of the labor it takes to get it. People have been enslaved for laboring in mines, and others have been killed for it. But here it is, we have planets that rain this stuff from the sky.

There are also asteroids made of gold as well. Can you imagine if one of those crashed the earth? It would probably upset the entire economy. Even though the earth has an abundance of supply, we have not even touched the resources of the cosmos. There is wealth everywhere! You just need to come into its same vibrational frequency.

Here we see a side of God we may not realize. God is flamboyant. He's flashy, and He's loud. It's not that He's trying to show off; this is just the way He is. If you look at the universe and all that goes on out there, you see bright stars, exoplanets, galaxies, and all kinds of colors, and there's still more to be discovered.

There's no end to God's supply in the universe. If God has a limitless supply of resources, why are so many broke people worldwide? This is because broke people have a broke mentality, and as a man thinketh, so is he.

GETTING RID OF THE OFFENSE

A broke mentality causes many people to get offended by wealth and riches, especially if the preacher is the one that has it. But God has made it possible for all of us to become rich in this life. You will never obtain that which you are offended by. People tend to dishonor what they're offended by, and we know this by scripture that where there's no honor, there will be no access. Many people are poor because they dishonor the biblical principles of wealth, and they dishonor those who have the wealth.

"Curse not the king, no not in thy thought; and curse not the rich in thy bedchamber: for a bird of the air shall carry the voice, and that which hath wings shall tell the matter." Ecclesiastes 10:20

We are told in scripture not to curse or speak against the rich. Those who are offended by rich people tend to give off negative energy that can be felt by those who are rich. You can't speak against where you want to be and expect the forces and laws that govern it to work for you. I used to be a young, hot-headed prophet who always spoke against prosperity preachers. The whole time I was speaking against them, I was broke.

It wasn't until the Lord corrected me and I repented

that I began to see prosperity explode in my life. People began to give to me, and I even ended up having favor with rich people. You will never have favor with the rich while speaking against riches. When I was speaking against the rich, they were living the life I desired deep down in my heart. It's easy to speak against something that you're not currently living.

I was more offended that they were living the life that I wasn't living, and their flamboyance only reminded me of where I wasn't in life. See, this is how offense causes you to see through dirty lenses. If anything, I should have been inspired to want to achieve more in life. Someone else's prosperity should inspire you and cause you to see that if they can do it, you can do it too. But first, you must get rid of your offense towards wealthy people.

I'm not saying that the rich are infallible or without error. And I'm not saying you must agree with everything they do. But to speak against who they are and their status in life will cause you to repel divine opportunities for wealth and success. I'm not a fan of most celebrities, but I admire their success stories. You must be humble enough to learn from the wealthy to be wealthy.

God desires for you to be blessed, but you must rid yourself of any offense towards riches, those who are rich, and having nice things. God desires that you own and possess the good of the land. Don't allow offense and a poverty mentality to rob you of this right.

5

The Elite Class

Now that we know that God wants us to be rich, we must understand that God has not called His people to live in the lower class. Just because Jesus said that the poor will always be among us doesn't mean that we have to fit in that classification. You are called to the upper class of the kingdom and in life. Some people say this has nothing to do with the gospel of salvation. But a thorough study of the word salvation will reveal that when God saved us, He saved our money too.

Salvation in Greek is the word "*sótéria*" (so-tay-ree'-ah), which means safety, deliverance, preservation, welfare, and PROSPERITY. That's right, Jesus also died and rose again for your soul and your prosperity. No one ever thought to connect their salvation to their money. But if Jesus saved your soul, then your soul should be prospering, and as scripture says, you will prosper as your soul prospers (3 John 1:2). So prosperity comes with the kingdom and salvation package.

This is not taught enough, which is why people either become or stay broke after giving their life to Jesus. Not only did Jesus die to save your soul, but He also died to break the curse of poverty off your life and save your money. Money changes your status and the way you live. It affords you the luxuries of life and reduces the stresses of debt and loss if you manage it right. Know that God wants to take you from ordinary to elite.

A CALL TO THE UPPER CLASS

"Now therefore, if ye will obey my voice indeed, and keep my covenant, then ye shall be a peculiar treasure unto me above all people: for all the earth is mine: And ye shall be unto me a kingdom of priests, and an holy nation. These are the words which thou shalt speak unto the children of Israel." Exodus 19:5,6

"For thou *art* an holy people unto the LORD thy God: the LORD thy God hath chosen thee to be a special people unto himself, above all people that *are* upon the face of the earth." Deuteronomy 7:6

When God delivered Israel from the bondage of slavery in Egypt, He intended to make them priests to the entire world. Originally, all twelve tribes were called to the priesthood until they grew impatient and started worshipping the golden calf when Moses went on the mountain to get the commandments. After that, the priesthood was taken from all of Israel and given to the tribe of Levi. But before that, it was God's original intent that all of Israel become the priesthood of the Lord. God desired to exalt His people above all people.

That may sound arrogant to the easily offendable, but this is God who we are talking about here. He loves all people, but He does not rank them equally. If you say you're a believer, God desires to place you above all that has not surrendered to Him. Jesus is head over everything to the church (Ephesians 1:22). This means that Jesus shares His authority over all things with the church.

Do you understand the gravity of this? Why are we not hearing this preached in our churches worldwide? Why are we so afraid to take our place on the earth? If wicked people can rule, then how much more are those who are righteous? Why are the richest people in the world unbelievers?

This should stand as a rebuke to every believer out there. God has called you to be superior, not in arrogance but in status. Scripture clearly states that the rich rule over the poor (Proverbs 22:7). Do you really think God wants anything or anyone else ruling over His people besides Him? And yet poverty is ruling many people, professed Christians included.

Scripture is clear on the status you are called to. You can either accept it or remain in a lower class of life. Either you are the head or the tail, above or below, the first or the last, the lender or the borrower. Choose this day which side of the fence you stand on. Stop thinking so low of yourself when God thinks highly of you.

You are His peculiar treasure above ALL PEOPLE. So why aren't you living like it? It's because a vast majority of our preachers have failed to teach you about reconciling your money with your salvation. We need to deal with the false humility that keeps people broke. Just because you're called to the upper class of living doesn't mean you should look down on the poor.

If anything, your status can help lift someone who is down. But you have to be up to lift someone else up. Greatness is a calling; if you are His, you're called to it.

GREATNESS STARTS FROM WITHIN

Everything you will do in life must first be processed and accepted within yourself. For you to be successful, your soul must first be prosperous. Your wealth is first within you. There's a such thing as the economy of the human anatomy. Everything that you will ever need in life to succeed, God placed it there.

This means that you and I are without excuse. Everything we need, we already have. All of us have something in us that will cause us to prosper if appropriately utilized.

"A man's gift maketh room for him, and bringeth him before great men." Proverbs 18:16

Did you know that the greatness in you will appeal to the greatness of others? Whatever gift God has given you is designed to bring you before people that have the power to upgrade and promote you. Are you working what God has given you? I can remember working in the ministry diligently for years with no major opportunities or doors opening for me. We can say all day long that it's not about the numbers, or we don't care if doors open for us or not.

But in reality, everything is measured by how much it grows. The average pastor will eventually become discouraged if he preached to empty chairs every Sunday for years. No one wants to dedicate their lives to something that isn't working. So if something is not working, then you must do it differently. Greatness is a seed that must be grown.

God has given us the ability to become great in our spheres of influence, responsibility, and calling. But we also must learn to honor the greatness of others. Now here's the second part of your gift making room for you. This is the most crucial part here. What you don't honor, you don't have access to. You must learn to invest in the relationships that will prosper you.

Gift in Hebrew is the word "matān" (mat-tawn') which means offering and presents. This word is also used when referring to giving gifts, offerings, and rewards. So not only do growing and working your inner greatness bring you before great people, your money and offerings do too. Now, this is where it gets controversial. I have seen crooked people apply this principle and become very successful.

This is one of those universal laws of success that works across the board for everyone. You must invest where you want to go in life or in ministry. If you don't believe enough in yourself to properly invest in yourself, then don't expect anyone else to believe in you. God places you around elite people when you're called to an elite class. But that access is not easily granted.

You'll have to put your pride to the side on this one. This is where you recognize the need for someone greater than yourself. You will not become great until you are promoted by someone greater. This is just how it goes, and it's the way God intended it to be. I am a chief apostle with my own network of leaders, and even I apply this.

When I'm around someone who is in a greater space than myself, I get reticent. I observe and listen, recognizing my privilege to be amid greatness. The people who say it doesn't take all of that are the same ones struggling right now. I'm not talking about tap dancing and kissing somebody's butt here. I'm talking about genuine honor for where you are trying to be.

So yes, your money and gifts do make room for you. How does it make room for you? Firstly, you invest where you are going by actually going. In other words, you pay to travel where they are. This includes gas money, hotels, flights, etc. You may say, "I don't have a lot of money."

But think about the amount of money you have spent in the past year alone on stuff you don't need. How many times have you eaten out instead of cooking at home? How many powerless prophetic services have you gone to and given hundreds or thousands of dollars? How many name-brand articles of clothing do you have in your closet? Your priorities are misplaced if you can afford a Louis Vuitton purse but can't afford a plane ticket and basic lodging.

I'm not telling you something that I haven't lived. My wife and I have traveled for hours to be a part of events where we were recognized and honored by those who had the power to promote us. I can remember my wife using her vacation time at work to travel to events and be among the examples of where we are trying to go. You will never get it until you learn to honor those who have it. How can God trust you with more money and resources when you can't even correctly steward what you have to help get you to where you're going?

Your gift will bring you before great people. Your money, presents, and rewards will cause great people to notice you. Believe me, when someone sows a significant seed, I notice. When someone constantly shows up to my services or meetings, I eventually notice them. When someone is constantly showing their support for me, I notice.

So if I notice, those who can promote you also notice. To prosper, you must first get it in your soul and work out your soul prosperity and money consciousness. Then you must get around people who walk in that status as much as you can. That's where you put your money up. And if you ever get a chance to come before great people, make sure you come with a gift.

In scripture, it was customary to come before prophets and rulers with gifts. You must learn to honor and appeal to greatness. Again, we are not talking about tap dancing and kissing butt. We are talking about genuine honor here. Wealth starts at the place of humility. So let your gift make room for you and bring you before great people.

WHY YOU MUST BE AROUND RICH PEOPLE

God wants your gift to make room for you and bring you before great people. When you come before great people, you have access to learn from them and be promoted by them. Yes, we all know that promotion comes from the Lord, but He still uses man to do it. Don't be silly! It will help if you rid yourself of the pride that makes you feel less than because of the greatness you are amongst.

Some things you will never learn from average people. When I say average, I'm not demeaning them as human beings. I'm speaking on their level of achievement or the lack thereof. Your company significantly shapes your character and influences your direction. Your company is a portrait of your future.

Some may say, "well, I don't have the priviledge of being around great people." And I would tell you that God is no respecter of persons. The same spiritual and universal laws work for everyone across the board. I don't care what no one says; the law of attraction works, and it's a biblical concept. I was one who had no wealthy connections.

No one in my family is a businessman or a millionaire. It wasn't until I started applying the principles I'm giving you in this book that I began to see significant fruit in my relationships and my money. As I began to agree with God and my desire to prosper, I applied these simple principles that eventually caused me to excel. But I had to get around those who had more and are more to get more. Don't let anyone make you feel guilty for investing in your future and changing your circle.

If you're called to the elite class in God, then you must get around elite people. You must get around those with the mind and the life you need. God brings you close to greatness before He makes you great. You will never be great until you start coming into the presence of the greats. Once your gift makes room for you and brings you before great people, you must learn how to become the least among the greats.

You always humble yourself under those who can promote you. Being the least among the greats is what will make you great. Great people only hang around their kind, and if you are repeatedly allowed access to them, they obviously see your greatness. You will be positioned for them to cultivate that in your character and your life. You must get around those who can change your life, which will require investment.

You're called to be an elite if you are reading this book. It's in you, so you're drawn to it. What I have outlined here are the necessary steps to greatness. I'm not telling you to kiss anyone behind here; I'm telling you to honor where you want to go and who you want to be. You will never be great settling for what's average. Elite status is calling your name. Will you answer?

6

The Wealth Of
The Wicked

When it comes to money, we must change our view about
it to possess it. Many treat abundance and money as
something evil just because wicked people have it. This
is a foolish assumption that keeps people broke. Everyone
drinks water, including wicked people. So does that make
water something wicked?

Of course not, but this is how we approach being rich
sometimes. If the wicked prosper, how much more should
the righteous prosper? Some evil people in the world have
a lot of money. These same people can do more than those
who say they're righteous because they have the resources
to do it. I have also discovered that many believers frown
upon living a certain lifestyle because the wicked or those
in the world live that life.

A pastor can't drive a Bentley without you thinking he's trying to be a celebrity. A preacher can't own a jet without you thinking he's robbing the church to pay for it. Such offenses at wealth need to be dealt with. You should want your pastor to ride in something nice and live comfortably. You should not want to sit under a broke and needy preacher.

You should also want this kind of life for yourself. There's enough wealth on this planet for all of us to live well. If evil people have no problem enjoying the abundance of God's provision on earth, you should desire even more to live that life.

UNIVERSAL PROVISION

"...for he maketh his sun to rise on the evil and on the good, and sendeth rain on the just and on the unjust." Matthew 5:45

Provision is available for everyone, even those we deem wicked. God provides even for those who are unjust. Think about that! Since God provides for the unjust, we can't be upset when they make wise moves with that provision. Those we deem wicked are usually those with the wisdom to produce wealth.

No human being on earth can't say that God is not a provider. The earth is full of resources. The major difference between the rich and the poor is the knowledge necessary to get the wealth. Money is neither good nor evil initially. Money takes on the nature of its handler.

Because money is neither good nor evil, that's how it has become a universal provision with universal access. So if the principles of provision are universal, there's no excuse for anyone being broke. Everyone has an equal opportunity to prosper. It doesn't matter what hand you were dealt in life. You can throw away the entire deck and get a new one just by renewing your mind.

"Behold the fowls of the air: for they sow not, neither do they reap, nor gather into barns; yet your heavenly Father feedeth them. Are ye not much better than they? Which of you by taking thought can add one cubit unto his stature? And why take ye thought for raiment? Consider the lilies of the field, how they grow; they toil not, neither do they spin: And yet I say unto you, That even Solomon in all his glory was not arrayed like one of these. Wherefore, if God so clothe the grass of the field, which to day is, and to morrow is cast into the oven, shall he not much more clothe you, O ye of little faith?" Matthew 6:26-30

Do you not see the universal provision here? According to what Jesus is saying here, there is provision even for those who don't sow. Now, this doesn't mean that you shouldn't give. There's a blessing of receiving and protection when we give. But God's resources and provision are so vast that it's available even at the basic level for those who don't give.

You and I are better than the lilies of the field, the birds of the air, and the grass of the field. If these things experience the limitless supply of provision and we are better, how much more should we receive, even at the lowest or most basic place in life? Don't get mad at the wicked because they understand universal provision and make the most out of it. Prosperity is God's provision, but our responsibility. There's no excuse for poverty other than willful ignorance.

FRIENDS OF UNRIGHTEOUS MAMMON

"And the lord commended the unjust steward, because he had done wisely: for the children of this world are in their generation wiser than the children of light. And I say unto you, Make to yourselves friends of the mammon of unrighteousness; that, when ye fail, they may receive you into everlasting habitations." Luke 16:8,9

Scripture says that the children of this world are wiser than the children of light. This scripture speaks in the context of handling money. When you want to learn to handle money, the people of this world have a better understanding. The scripture mentioned is part of a parable Jesus gave about a rich man who heard accusations about his steward wasting the rich man's goods. So the rich man summoned his steward to give an account of all of his dealing because he was about to be fired.

The steward did something very shrewd to secure his position. He called his master's debtors one by one. Once he found out what these debtors owed his master, the steward made them put a hefty down payment on their debt. He took the initiative to recover his master's debt. This impressed the rich man, and he commended the steward for it.

But why exactly was the steward commended? Because he got his master's money back in the rotation. See, money is never supposed to stay still. Money should always be moving and working for you. You lose money when your money is not moving.

This is why we need to make friends with unrighteous mammon. In other words, we need to become acquainted with how money operates and how money moves. The rich master stopped making money because his money wasn't moving in rotation. This is why the steward came under scrutiny. Rich people understand that you have to always make sure your money is working for you to stay rich.

If your money stops working for you, you will eventually return to working for money. You must make friends or become acquainted with how money works. You must learn what it takes to get money moving and working for you. This is how people (including the wicked) prosper. The steward was also labeled as unjust.

He was unjust because he didn't handle his master's money right. But he was wise because he knew what it took to get his master's money moving. Wicked people prosper because they simply understand money. They're wise enough to study it and discipline their habits to master it. I find that church people can be some of the laziest and scariest people you'll ever meet.

They demonize everything and everyone outside of the four walls of their building, but they're needier than the people they criticize. Imagine that! Criticizing the people that are in a greater space than you or who could help you can cause money to be repelled from you. This is why scripture tells us not to speak against the rich (Ecclesiastes 10:20). You actually need the rich to like you.

Promotion usually comes from those greater than you and more affluent than you. Whether they're saved or not, God will use anybody to upgrade your status and standard of living. How we view money and those who have it must change. Scripture proves that the unjust and unrighteous are better at using money than those who say they serve God. Did you know God judges how you handle money? We will cover this more in the next chapter.

UNIVERSAL WISDOM

"If any of you lack wisdom, let him ask of God, that giveth to all men liberally, and upbraideth not; and it shall be given him. But let him ask in faith, nothing wavering. For he that wavereth is like a wave of the sea driven with the wind and tossed." James 1:5,6

If you are broke, don't just ask for the money. First, ask for the wisdom to obtain and steward it. If you lack wisdom, scripture tells you to ask God for it. But look at what it says after we are told to ask God for wisdom. Next, it says that God gives wisdom to all men, and He doesn't upbraid (scold or criticize) those He gives His wisdom to. God gives His wisdom to all men, not just "saved" men.

There's no criticism or condemnation of any kind when it comes to the wisdom of God. He will place His wisdom in the hands of evildoers if that individual is going to accomplish the endgame of what God intends to produce. Many believers are broke because they expect their financial wisdom to come from the pulpit. Meanwhile, the pastor is just as broke as they are most of the time. This is one of the many reasons why our spiritual leaders need to become wealthy.

Unless your pastor is legitimately rich and knows how to teach others how to get there effectively, you will most likely get your financial wisdom outside of the church. Church people tend to think that if it's not in church, then it's not from God. But as we can see, His wisdom is given to all people. This understanding alone could cause you to heed the right voice that can bring you to financial freedom. So when it comes to wealth and riches, sometimes your financial success is in the voice of someone you wouldn't usually listen to.

WICKED PLACES, WICKED SPACES

We have already established that God wants you to possess the wealth of the wicked. That means your money is probably in spaces you wouldn't want to venture into. If you want to be rich, you can't be afraid of corruption. You should be so solid within yourself that a certain amount of cash can't easily sway your morals. Money doesn't always change who you are; it usually enhances who you are already.

The financial industry is a very corrupt and biased one. However, the principle and opportunities for success are universal. Everyone has the chance to prosper, but you must know how to be in environments and among certain people.

"Behold, I send you forth as sheep in the midst of wolves: be ye therefore wise as serpents, and harmless as doves." Matthew 10:16

In a day and age where church people are trying to escape wickedness, here it is Jesus telling the apostles that He will place them right in the middle of it. We are to be like sheep among wolves. In other words, we have to learn to maintain innocence in our character while dominating the sphere God assigned us to. God will place you among wolves to accomplish what He wants. You don't have to become a wolf to compete with them and outdo them.

Jesus also told His apostles to be wise as serpents and harmless as doves. This means that you must again maintain proper character while using the wisdom of the serpent. We must learn to become wise as serpents without becoming serpents. God has a habit of placing His people in the midst of influential wickedness just to rise in the ranks and outdo everyone. Is this not what He did with the prophet Daniel?

When Babylon captured Israel, Daniel rose up in rank prophetically and governmentally. This was so much to where he became number one over the astrologers and dream interpreters. Daniel also became the second man and top president in the empire. God doesn't just want you rich; He wants you to have influence. It's the wealthy that has influence.

To have influence, you must be in influential spaces. As a prophet, Daniel had top spots in Babylon's spiritual and political spheres. Though scripture doesn't say much about it, much wealth and riches came with Daniel's positions. Wealth gives you influence and causes influential people to notice and even favor you. Remember, a man's gift makes room for him to bring him before great people.

Many times, those great people occupy wicked spaces. Babylon was a wicked nation, yet a prophet thrived in more than one area. Daniel stood his ground, even when his devotion to God was under attack, and God rescued him from the Lion's den. After that, even the king began to acknowledge the God of Israel. Daniel was favored and beloved by the king of Babylon.

God also wants to give you special favor in high places. These people may not serve your God, but they still serve His purpose. God places you in such environments to secure His purpose in that space. Don't miss your wealth being super religious about environments God wants to give you influence in. Your money is greatly attached to whatever area God wants to give you influence in.

If there are evil rich people in the world, God wants His people to be richer. God's people are supposed to be above all people (Deuteronomy 7:6). Riches are included in this. God will never let an adversary outdo Him. He just desires more people to grab hold of the revelation of riches and why God wants us to be rich.

"And I will give thee the treasures of darkness, and

hidden riches of secret places, that thou mayest know that I, the LORD, which call thee by thy name, am the God of Israel." Isaiah 45:3

Think on these things!

7

Mystery of Stewardship

Now that we can biblically grasp the concept of wealth and riches being a godly thing, we must also understand that we have a responsibility to maintain it. I have come to discover that your faith can produce riches, but it's your stewardship that causes you to keep it. How can someone win millions of dollars in the lottery and lose it all five years later? They were poor stewards, and their greed caused them to live above their means. Keeping money is more complex than making it if you don't know what you're doing.

We have an individual responsibility to take care of what we have. Just because you have it doesn't mean you should overspend it. Scripture outlines how we are rewarded for being good stewards. The first thing we must understand about stewardship is that we must be able to adequately produce. This comes because of not being slothful in business.

NO MORE SLACK HANDS

"He becometh poor that dealeth *with* a slack hand: but the hand of the diligent maketh rich." Proverbs 10:4

To get out of poverty, you must find something lucrative to become diligent in. Lazy people make poor stewards. Therefore, such individuals become complacent and never set out to achieve more than what they have limited themselves to. There's a saying, "work smart, not hard." I strongly believe in this; however, working smart still requires work and diligence.

Scripture is clear that diligent people are those who become rich. Those who find something worth sticking to and working on see fruit in what they're doing. Diligent people don't give up! Setbacks and failures don't discourage them. Diligent people always find a way to make something work even if they have to change some things around.

Poor people are those who refuse to try or those who don't keep trying. Every human being has an ability from God to prosper. Working that ability and perfecting it determines whether you will prosper. To steward wealth and riches properly, you must be able to accumulate enough wealth to manage appropriately. This also requires you to learn money management principles and how money flows in your generation.

Romans 12:11 tells us not to be slothful in business. This means that we must take our business seriously. When you take your business seriously, you become diligent and undistracted. To gain money, we must take business and money seriously. Most business people are serious about their business and how they manage and dispense their money.

This is because they know what it takes to make money and keep it flowing. Since funding for their livelihood is secure, they can continue to help humanity. There's a blessing in being diligent. It's the diligence that gets results.

PROVISION IS A COMMANDMENT

"But if any provide not for his own, and specially for those of his own house, he hath denied the faith, and is worse than an infidel." 1 Timothy 5:8

Did you know that the word commands us to provide for our own households? All of us have a duty to our own households to provide financially for our immediate families. You can only access provision when you're diligent enough to put in the work. But with this work comes a grace to get it done. Remember, provision is a promise and a covenant right. So if this promise and covenant right is a commandment, then it also needs to be a priority.

God cares about our ability to produce wealth. He would not have allowed it to be included in scripture if He didn't. Why would God want you to have a family that you can't adequately provide for? We must change how we view money and study what God says about it. An accurate study of money and provision will show you how godly wealth is.

According to scripture, it's bad when you can't provide for yourself or your own family. The apostle Paul said that you're worse than an unbeliever. Some don't believe in God or Jesus and provide for their households better than professed believers. The world should not be outshining the church in this area. We should be wealthier than the world!

Poverty alone will ruin much of our witness to the world. Sure, you may be able to supplement that with signs, wonders, miracles, and prophetic ministry. But eventually, people want to see how you're living. This is why we must change our minds about money. God commands you to produce, and He has made it possible for you to do so.

GOOD STEWARDSHIP VS. POOR STEWARDSHIP

"For the kingdom of heaven is as a man travelling into a far country, who called his own servants, and delivered unto them his goods. And unto one he gave five talents, to another two, and to another one; to every man according to his several ability; and straightway took his journey. Then he that had received the five talents went and traded with the same, and made them other five talents. And likewise he that had received two, he also gained other two. But he that had received one went and digged in the earth, and hid his lord's money. After a long time the lord of those servants cometh, and reckoneth with them. And so he that had received five talents came and brought other five talents, saying, Lord, thou deliveredst unto me five talents: behold, I have gained beside them five talents more. His lord said unto him, Well done, thou good and faithful servant: thou hast been faithful over a few things, I will make thee ruler over many things: enter thou into the joy of thy lord. He also that had received two talents came and said, Lord, thou deliveredst unto me two talents: behold, I have gained two other talents beside them. His lord said unto him, Well done, good and faithful servant; thou hast been faithful over a few things, I will make thee ruler over many things: enter thou into the joy of thy lord. Then he which had received the one talent came and said, Lord, I knew thee that thou art an hard man, reaping where thou hast not sown, and gathering where thou hast not strawed: And I was afraid, and went and hid thy talent in the earth: lo, there thou hast that is thine. His lord answered and said unto him, Thou wicked and slothful servant, thou knewest that I reap where I sowed not, and gather where I have not strawed: Thou oughtest therefore to have put my money to the exchangers, and then at my coming I should have received mine own with usury. Take therefore the talent from him, and give it unto him which hath ten talents. For unto every one that hath shall be given, and he shall have abundance: but from him that hath not shall be taken away even that which he hath. And cast ye the unprofitable servant into outer darkness: there shall be weeping and gnashing of teeth." Matthew 25:14-30

This passage shows how God feels about money and how we handle it. In this parable, we see a ruler going away for a while. But before he does, he calls his servants over to him. He gives each of them talents (money) that he expects them to double while he's away. He gave one servant five talents, two talents to the second one, and one talent to the third servant.

He gave each servant talents according to their own ability. The ruler didn't set them up to fail but to succeed. The servants with the five and two talents doubled their master's money. The servant with the one talent hid his money and did nothing with it—the first two servants were called good and faithful.

They were faithful over the few or the little that the master gave them. As a result, they were promoted to rule over more. How you handle the little determines how God trusts you with more. Your ability to multiply the little determines how God invests in you with more. This is how God sees you when you properly steward your money.

He expects you to at least double what you have before He can trust you with more. We often pray for more money when we are poor stewards of our little money. What you do with the least determines if God will trust you with abundance. This is a universal principle here. God will never promote you if you cannot handle the little money that you have.

Rich people are those who can take the little and make it much. It's not always that you need more money. You need to learn how money works and use that to multiply the little money that you have. This is how the least becomes the greatest. Good and faithful servants to the Lord are those who know how to multiply money.

How you handle money determines how God labels you. The first two servants could enter the joy of the Lord. If there's no joy in your life, it could be because you are a poor or unjust steward. Remember, Jesus is describing how the kingdom of God operates here. This is a parable about the kingdom of heaven.

Heaven judges how you handle money. Money speaks a lot as it pertains to the spiritual world. Most people don't even realize the spiritual force of money and what it communicates to eternity and the spiritual world. That's a different lesson and another book altogether, but we must understand that money is spiritual. Spiritually matured people know how to handle it properly.

Now, look at what the master told the servant who hid his money and did nothing with it. This man was called wicked and slothful. But listen to his excuse for why he did nothing with the money his master gave him. He told his master that he knew he was a hard man reaping where he had not sown. In other words, he judged how his master made his money and conducted his business. This tells us he had a critical opinion of the wealthy.

This usually comes from jealousy, insecurity, and inferiority complexes. Those who are critical of the rich rarely take the risks or steps to become rich themselves. When you curse the rich, you curse your future. Therefore, scripture tells us not to curse the rich

(Ecclesiastes 10:20). You will never get to where you need to be speaking against people who are already there.

Instead of increasing the money given to him, this servant remained in fear and criticize his masters' wealth. He spoke against a system he didn't understand but was being introduced to through his master. Poor stewards are great at criticizing, which keeps them out of any realm of influence God may have for them. Let us examine what happens to this wicked and slothful servant next. Verse 28 tells us that the talent he had was taken from him and given to the servant that produced the most.

Have you noticed that those who produce the most continue to increase? I'm revealing a universal law here. This is one of the reasons why the rich get richer and the poor get poorer. The rich continue to produce more while the poor hang on to their little. The servant with the least said that he was afraid.

When you are afraid, you go into survival mode. People with this mentality will never become rich because it's all about self-preservation. These types of people will never take the chances and step out on faith to produce the life they desire. And yet they will be the most critical of how others get their wealth. What if this unprofitable servant focused on his ability to produce instead of his fears and critiquing how his master made his money? With stewardship, instead of critiquing those who are already there, learn and glean from their experience.

GOD WANTS TO PROFIT OFF YOU

One major issue we have with prosperity is that we don't see God as a businessman. Where do you think the whole concept of business came from? Indeed the devil didn't create it. Because God is not a hypocrite, He first becomes a thing before He sets it in place as a standard for others. God is the first partaker of His own divine nature.

The same is valid for business. Scripture even shows us that Lucifer was a businessman in heaven before He fell. So it says that he had a multitude of merchandise (Ezekiel 28:16). Lucifer used his business influence to promote violence and revolt in heaven. It makes you rethink what heaven was like during that time and what heaven will be like when we go there.

By definition, merchandise is goods to be bought and sold. So Lucifer had a multitude of businesses when he was in heaven. Outside of him being a cherub, this would also give him tremendous influence among the heavenly host. Because his voice was already trusted, he used that trust to turn hearts away from the Lord. We must understand that everything on earth was first in heaven.

So when we preach the kingdom of God, our preaching is incomplete until we get a revelation of all that is in heaven. Thy kingdom come is more than just the supernatural and revival. We also need to include riches in that message, too. God doesn't just want you saved; He wants you to prosper. As a businessman Himself, God also wants to profit from you.

For Lucifer to become a businessman, God first had to become one. All of heaven and creation are the extension of who God is. For Lucifer to become a businessman, God first had to be a businessman, being that He's the one who established the institution from the beginning. It really makes you rethink who God is in totality. He is everything that He tells us to be.

If God is a businessman and created the institution of business from the beginning, how are you bringing profit to God and His kingdom? We think money doesn't matter, but you can't do business without currency. Money is a medium of exchange. You exchange goods and services according to its correct value.

Money is one of the ways you weigh the value and honor of something or someone. So if there is business in heaven, then there's also money in heaven, too. This is why money is important to God and the spiritual world overall. How you handle money determines how God handles you. Do you now see why stewardship is so important?

If you make God no profit, He has no further use for you. This has nothing to do with His love for you. It has everything to do with His business and your employment in His business. There are plenty of people I love dearly, but I can't do business with them because they are unprofitable in that area. As we see in the parable aforementioned, if God seeks to employ you and you don't produce, then you are wicked, slothful, and unprofitable.

If you work for God, He expects you to produce, especially because He has already given you the ability to get wealth and only gives you what you can handle.

God expects you to produce wealth for the kingdom. The kingdom can't expand without it. Miracles will only get you, but so far. It's time out for having miracles without resources.

Therefore you must learn to steward the little you have so that God can profit more from you. God has placed within everyone the ability to prosper, and He expects a return on His investment. At the end of our lives, all of us will be judged according to how profitable we were to God. We will be judged by how we handle God's business and God's money. The subject of money is a serious one to God.

It's so serious that Ananias and Sapphira lost their lives for being stingy with their money. God is a God of money! He cares how it circulates in the earth and His kingdom among His people. So how have you profited God lately? We must change our minds about money to get things done on the earth.

There's no sin in having a lot of money. The sin we need to be concerned with is greed, along with being stingy. Greedy and stingy people are ruled by mammon. Such people cannot inherit the kingdom of God. God desires that we be wise but generous with our money.

You must have more to give more. God can't profit from your life if you're poor and lacking. Though God cares about the poor and how we treat them, the best way to help the poor is to become rich. You can't bring anyone else out of a state of being that you're still in. So again, in conclusion, the best stewards get the more excellent seats in the kingdom.

Your position in God is determined by how trusted you are in handling His resources. Therefore the rich get richer, and the poor get poorer. So are you a good and faithful servant of the Lord? Or are you a wicked, slothful, and unprofitable servant? Choose this day which one you want to be.

Printed in Great Britain
by Amazon

40318146R00046